The Bowling Trivia Book

BY DONALD WILLIAMS

To:
Victoria, Felice, and Denise,
grandmother, mother, and wife,
thank you many times, for many things;

L.S. for being a true friend;

and to the thousands of bowlers,
as well as the hundreds of bowling proprietors,
whom I have had the pleasure of knowing.

Contents

Foreword

Bowling is an activity for everyone. Young or old, first time or seasoned professional, all can participate.

Whether it's watching a televised match in which thousands of dollars are at stake or seeing a physically challenged bowler knock down a few pins, either can be a joy to watch.

Seventy-nine million bowlers visit thousands of bowling centers at least once a year. Hopefully, this book will expose the deep spirit of the game and promote the real by-product that comes from bowling — **FUN!**

FRAME 1:
A Colorful History

The earliest known objects used for a game similar to bowling date from 5200 B.C. Where were these objects found?

IN THE TOMB OF AN EGYPTIAN BOY BY SCIENTIST SIR FLINDERS PETRIE DURING THE 1930'S.

An ancient Polynesian game in which the players rolled round stones at pins was called Ula Maika. This game has a unique similarity to modern bowling. What is this similarity?

THE DISTANCE BETWEEN THE BALL AND PINS USED IN ULA MAIKA WAS 60 FEET. THIS IS BASICALLY THE SAME AS TODAY'S SPECIFICATIONS.

When bowling at pins was popular in Germany, the participants did not consider the activity a sport. In what ceremony was bowling included?

MANY HISTORIANS BELIEVE BOWLING AT PINS WAS AN ACTIVITY THAT WAS INCLUDED IN RELIGIOUS RITES.

What German cleric settled on nine as the number of pins for early versions of Kegeling or bowling?

MARTIN LUTHER.

There is a section of land known as Bowling Green in Manhattan. How did the name of this area originate?

LAWN BOWLING WAS PLAYED BY BRITISH SETTLERS IN THIS AREA.

Remember the story of Rip Van Winkle who fell asleep for a very long time? What were the circumstances that led to Rip Van Winkle going into a long sleep?
HE DRANK FROM A KEG BELONGING TO A BAND OF LITTLE MEN WHO WERE PLAYING NINEPINS.

What royal decree did King Henry VIII issue in 1541?
ALL FORMS OF BOWLING WERE OUTLAWED IN ENGLAND.

When Henry VIII outlawed bowling, he gave three reasons for his actions. What were they?
HE BELIEVED THAT BOWLING HAD BECOME A VICIOUS FORM OF GAMBLING; HIS SOLDIERS WERE SPENDING TOO MUCH TIME BOWLING; AND HE BELIEVED BOWLING WAS ONLY A PRIVILEGE OF THE WEALTHY.

What was the name of the first organization in the United States that attempted to regulate tenpin bowling?
THE NATIONAL BOWLING ASSOCIATION.

In what year was the National Bowling Association formed?
1875.

In 1890, which short-lived organization followed the National Bowling Association?
THE AMERICAN BOWLING LEAGUE.

In what year was the Professional Bowlers Association organized?

1958.

Who was the inventor of the first automatic pinsetter to meet sanctioned approval?

GOTTFRIED SCHMIDT.

This automatic pinsetter was first displayed at a tournament in Buffalo, New York. In what year was this ?

1946.

This machine was not officially approved until 1952, when 12 machines were installed in a Midwestern city. Name the city that first received these machines.

MT. CLEMENS, MICHIGAN.

What was the name of the bowling center in which these machines were installed?

THE BOWL O DROME.

In what year did the Olympic games offer bowling competition?

IN 1936 IN BERLIN, GERMANY.

What American bowler won all bowling events during the 1936 Olympic competition?

HANK MARINO.

In 1942, a bowling group was organized to provide recreational equipment for servicemen and also to raise funds for veterans programs. What was the name of this dedicated group?

THE BOWLERS VICTORY LEGION.

What occurred in the early 1840's that began a meteoric rise in the popularity of bowling?

INDOOR LANES OR ALLEYS APPEARED, THEREBY NEGATING WEATHER AS A FACTOR.

Women bowlers participated in programs to raise money for the armed services during World War II. One of these projects raised money to fund a Douglas Attack Bomber. Because of their efforts, what was this airplane named?

MISS WIBC, AFTER THE WOMEN'S INTERNATIONAL BOWLING CONGRESS.

In what year was the American Bowling Congress formed?

1895.

In what year did the American Bowling Congress organize the first U.S. national bowling tournament?
1901.

In 1932, bowling proprietors from eight states gathered in Detroit for a meeting. What was created by these bowling establishment owners that continues to this day?
THE BOWLING PROPRIETORS ASSOCIATION OF AMERICA WAS FORMED.

While King Henry VIII was a resident of Whitehall Palace in the 1500's, he made several additions to this residence. What did he specifically create space for?
HE MADE SPACE TO ACCOMMODATE INDOOR BOWLING.

King Henry's daughter, Elizabeth I, continued to recognize bowling as a status symbol among the elite. What game did the nobility of the times play regularly at their estates?
SKITTLES. MANY HAD SPECIFIC SKITTLE AREAS AT THEIR ESTATES.

In January of 1841, an edition of the Hartford Daily Curant ran a story about a Grogshop or tavern. With this story came a specific "first." What was it?
THIS GROGSHOP INCLUDED A TENPIN ALLEY IN FULL OPERATION, WHICH IS POSSIBLY THE VERY FIRST PUBLISHED REFERENCE TO THE GAME OF TENPINS.

During the early 1300's in Germany, approval was given to bowling games. This opened the sport to many people, allowing it to eventually become part of village festivals. Who granted this endorsement?

THE CATHOLIC CHURCH.

Many credit three contributing factors — all beginning with the letter "A" — for upgrading and expanding the image of bowling. The first is automation. What are the other two?

ARCHITECTURE AND AIR CONDITIONING.

McCook Bowl in Dayton, Ohio was considered a marvel of engineering because of what reason?

THIS BOWLING CENTER HAD 44 LANES WITHOUT A VERTICAL SUPPORT POST IN THE BOWLING LANE AREA.

During the 1941–42 season, a national war bond tournament was held. What was the name of this tournament that was displayed on posters in many bowling centers?

KEEP 'EM ROLLIN'. IT WAS A SLOGAN TO SUPPORT OUR MILITARY DURING WORLD WAR II.

In what year was the Women's International Bowling Congress founded?

1916.

In the early days of bowling, what score was considered a perfect game?

200.

In the early days of American Bowling Congress Tournaments, what prizes were used to reward winners?

THEIR PRIZE WINNINGS WERE PAID IN GOLD COINS.

John McGraw and Wilbert Robinson were baseball people who also became bowling proprietors. What tenpin-related bowling game did these gentlemen create?

THEY CREATED THE GAME OF DUCK PINS BY TURNING DOWN SOME OF THEIR PINS AND REDUCING THE SIZE OF THE BOWLING BALLS.

This game grew so popular that a National Duck Pin Bowling Congress was organized. In what year was this association started?

1927.

The original meeting to establish the American Bowling Congress was held in a building known as Beethoven Hall. Prior to this historic meeting, what other bowling business had been conducted in Beethoven Hall?

THIS NEW YORK CITY BUILDING WAS THE HEADQUARTERS OF THE UNITED BOWLING CLUBS.

Every bowler who donated to the Bowlers Victory Legion received a gift of an embroidered emblem. What two words adorned this symbolic patch?

ALONG WITH THE BVL LOGO WERE THE WORDS "I GAVE."

During World War II, posters asking bowlers to "Bowl over the Axis" encouraged the purchase of war bonds. What were some of the items that could be funded with war bond purchases?

WAR BONDS TOTALING $500,000 ALLOWED THE DONOR TO NAME A HEAVY BOMBER; $150,000 IN BONDS WOULD NAME A PURSUIT SHIP; AND $75,000 IN BONDS WOULD SPONSOR A TANK.

The Women's International Bowling Congress raised funds to purchase several war planes during World War II. In 1944, what was the name of the campaign by the WIBC that led to the purchase of an ambulance plane?

THE WINGS OF MERCY.

In October of 1943, the National Bowling Congress was formed in Chicago. It was made up of bowling proprietors, officials of the American Bowling Congress, and representatives of bowling manufacturers. What crisis brought this organization together?

THE UNITED STATES GOVERNMENT PROPOSED INSTITUTING A TAX ON BOWLING.

In 1941, the American Bowling Congress took a patriotic step that affected thousands of bowlers. What did the ABC do?

THE ABC PROVIDED, FREE OF CHARGE, SANCTIONING AND CERTIFICATION TO ALL LEAGUES, BOWLERS, AND ESTABLISHMENTS OF THE ARMED SERVICES.

In what year were the current headquarters of the American Bowling Congress located in Milwaukee, Wisconsin built?

1952. AN EXPANSION WAS ADDED IN 1961.

Because of the critical labor shortages during World War II, many bowling centers were forced to close their doors. A shortage of what type of employee was critical to a bowling center's operation?

BEFORE THE INVENTION OF AUTOMATED EQUIPMENT, PIN BOYS WERE A NECESSITY TO STAY IN BUSINESS.

FRAME 2:
It's Showtime

In 1975, there was a popular television show known as the "Superstars Competition." Athletes from many different sports competed for prize money. What "superstar" contestant credited his victory in bowling as the key to winning the overall competition?

O.J. SIMPSON.

In 1960, NBC produced a national bowling television show. Name the show.

"JACKPOT BOWLING."

Who was the comedian who hosted the television show "Jackpot Bowling?"

MILTON BERLE.

In the recent movie "The Flintstones," what was the name of the bowling center that Fred and Barney frequented?

THE BEDROCK BOWL O RAMA.

Fred Flintstone and Barney Rubble were on the same bowling team. What was the name of their team?

THE WATER BUFFALOS.

Name the movie whose story line featured the rags-to-riches tale of a professional bowler?

THIS 1979 RELEASE WAS TITLED "DREAMER."

Name the actor who portrayed the professional bowler in the movie "Dreamer."

TIM MATHESON.

A movie distributed by Columbia Pictures titled "Ten Pin Magic" was a truly unique bowling movie at the time. Why?

"TEN PIN MAGIC" FEATURED AUTOMATIC PINSETTERS.

Can you name at least three television sitcoms that featured episodes that took place in a bowling center?

"THE HONEYMOONERS," "ALL IN THE FAMILY," "ROSEANNE," "LAVERNE AND SHIRLEY," AND "THE ANDY GRIFFITH SHOW" WOULD ALL QUALIFY.

What was the name of the popular television bowling show that featured local viewers as contestants competing for cash prizes?

"BOWLING FOR DOLLARS."

In April of 1950, a "bowling theme song" was introduced at the 47TH American Bowling Congress Championships. What was the name of this bowling song?

"ROLL ON," WHICH WAS WRITTEN BY ERV. CRAIG.

The members of this traveling group were involved in a transcontinental bowling league that competed in cities the group visited. What famous entertainment troup in the 1940's participated in this unique cross-country league?
THE ICE FOLLIES.

Radio station WXYZ in Detroit, Michigan featured a bowling show called "The 10 Pin Talker." Who was the host of this popular show?
FRED WOLF.

In the famous comic strip "Peanuts," what nickname did Snoopy use while bowling?
JOE SANDBAGGER.

To the dismay of his bowling buddies, what was Joe Sandbagger's bowling average?
ONE.

Who was the first professional bowler to appear on the "Ed Sullivan Show?"
WAYNE ZAHN.

On the very popular "The Andy Griffith Show," which Mayberry resident bowled a 300 game?
HOWARD SPRAGUE, WHILE HE WAS A MEMBER OF THE MAYBERRY BOWLING TEAM.

Who were the other members of the Mayberry team?
HOWARD BOWLED WITH ANDY TAYLOR AND GOOBER PYLE.

Who was the sponsor of the Mayberry bowling team?
EMMETT CLARK'S FIX IT SHOP.

Andy Taylor also bowled in another league from time to time. What was the name of this league?
THE PEACE OFFICERS LEAGUE.

Archie Bunker bowled during several episodes of "All In The Family." During an episode that aired December 16, 1972, what bowling team did Archie try to join?
THE CANNONBALLERS.

Why did Archie not make the team?
HE WAS BLACKBALLED IN ORDER TO ALLOW ANOTHER PLAYER TO TAKE HIS PLACE ON THE TEAM.

What connection does the television cartoon show "The Simpsons" have with bowling?
DURING ONE EPISODE, THE ENTIRE SIMPSON FAMILY TRAVELED TO ST. LOUIS TO VISIT THE NATIONAL BOWLING HALL OF FAME.

With what special souvenir did the Simpson family leave the Hall of Fame?

THEY HAD A FAMILY PICTURE TAKEN IN FRONT OF THE BOWLING PIN CAR ON DISPLAY IN THE HALL OF FAME.

On the television show "The Honeymooners," Ralph Cramden was a member of what bowling team?

THE RACCOON LODGE TEAM.

In what city did Ralph Cramden and Ed Norton bowl most often on the television show "The Honeymooners?"

BROOKLYN, NEW YORK.

This television female comedy duo often frequented bowling centers. One of the characters always had her initial embroidered on her bowling shirts. Who were these ladies?

LAVERNE AND SHIRLEY.

In 1934, during a magazine interview, Ginger Rogers listed bowling as one of her two favorite leisure activities. What was the other activity?

HORSEBACK RIDING.

NBC once televised a popular morning quiz show called "Say When." This show was seen by more than a million viewers. What bowling product was offered as a prize to the contestants on this show?

A WARDROBE OF DEXTER BOWLING SHOES.

The world-famous Vienna Boys Choir were present at a bowling related event in 1961. With what event were they involved?

THEY PERFORMED AT THE OPENING OF A NEW BOWLING CENTER IN AUSTRIA.

Can you name the professional bowler who appeared on the televised game show "To Tell the Truth?"

BILL BATTISTA.

In 1934, MGM Studios produced a bowling movie. What was the title of that movie?

"STRIKES AND SPARES."

This movie starred Andy Veripapa, in which he bowled trick shot after trick shot. What famous Veripapa trick shot performed in this movie was known as the "tunnel shot?"

TO PICK UP A ONE PIN SPARE, HE BOWLED THROUGH THE LEGS OF 10 SHOWGIRLS STANDING ON THE LANE.

In 1944, the motion picture "Since You Went Away" was produced starring Robert Walker and Jennifer Jones. What reason did the producer give for including bowling scenes in this movie?

IT WAS A STORY OF THE AMERICAN HOME FRONT DURING THE WAR AND THE PRODUCER THOUGHT THAT BOWLING WAS AN INTEGRAL PART OF EVERYDAY LIFE DURING THIS TIME.

FRAME 3:
It's True

What branch of the U.S. Military issued a unit patch that featured a bowling ball knocking down pins?

U.S. ARMY 19TH BOMBARDMENT SQUADRON.

How much pressure impacts the lane when a 16-pound bowling ball meets the surface?

APPROXIMATELY 1,800 POUNDS PER SQUARE INCH.

The National Sanitary Sales company distributed this rather unique product during the 1950's with a bowling motif on the package. You will never guess this one.

"SPARES" PROPHYLACTICS INCLUDED BOWLING BALL AND PIN ARTWORK ON THE PACKAGE.

For a bowling team who competed in 1966, the number "1950" had special meaning. What did this number represent?

IT WAS THE COMBINED WEIGHT OF THE FIVE-MAN TEAM. THEIR INDIVIDUAL WEIGHTS WERE 300, 365, 473, 366, AND 446.

In 1991, what personality starred in a bowling comedy video called "Life in the Bowling Lane?"

THIS UNRATED VIDEOTAPE STARRED "THE UNKNOWN COMIC."

In October of 1954, what well-known magazine wrote a negative article about bowling titled "The Sport That Ruins Youngsters?"

"REDBOOK" MAGAZINE. THE STORY DISCUSSED PROBLEMS INVOLVING PIN BOYS.

As of 1993, how many people are estimated to participate in all forms of bowling worldwide?

MORE THAN 110 MILLION PEOPLE, IN MORE THAN 80 COUNTRIES.

Bowling hustlers sometimes use illegally weighted bowling balls to gain an unfair scoring advantage. They drill holes in balls and fill them with a heavy substance. These are called Dodo balls. What would you be referring to when discussing a 7-9 Dodo ball?

UNSCRUPULOUS BOWLERS WOULD CEMENT HALF OF A SEVEN POUND BALL TO A HALF OF A NINE POUND BALL. THE RESULTING BALL WOULD "CLIMB" INTO THE POCKET.

What major liquor company produced a glass liquor decanter in the shape of a bowling pin?

IN 1958, THE JIM BEAM DISTILLERY PRODUCED THESE COLLECTIBLE DECANTERS TO DISTRIBUTE THEIR BOURBON.

What was the betting line the first time a Las Vegas casino accepted bets on a Professional Bowlers Association event?

FOUR-TO-ONE ODDS WERE GIVEN THAT PETE WEBER WOULD WIN.

In what year were these odds offered?

1985.

How many games are bowled each day around the globe?

OVER SEVEN MILLION GAMES ARE BOWLED EACH DAY.

On average, how many visits do American bowlers make to bowling centers each week?

ABOUT 14 MILLION VISITS EACH WEEK.

Including men, women, and children, how many Americans participate in sanctioned, organized competition?

APPROXIMATELY 6.1 MILLION ANNUALLY.

What is the world record for stacking bowling balls on top of each other?

AS OF 1989, THE RECORD STOOD AT NINE.

What are the odds that you will bowl a 300 game on your next attempt?

TWENTY-SIX THOUSAND TO ONE.

In what country will you find the world's largest bowling center?

JAPAN.

How many lanes does this bowling center have?

THE CENTER HAS 141 LANES. THE TOKYO WORLD LANES CENTER, NOW CLOSED, HAD 252 LANES.

A bowling pin car is on display at the National Bowling Hall of Fame. It was built for promotional purposes by an Ohio bowling proprietor in the early 1940's. What make of automobile was the foundation for this unique vehicle?
A STUDEBAKER.

How much money was the proprietor of the car offered for its purchase and the accompanying patent rights?
IN EXCESS OF $10,000.

The Bowling Pin Car has a license plate that shouldn't surprise you. What does this plate say?
GO-BOWL.

In 1943, you could purchase a product, through the bowling magazines, intended for league secretaries. It cost one dollar. What was this essential product that was years ahead of its time?
THE "ALL PURPOSE BOWLING CALCULATOR" COULD FIGURE INDIVIDUAL AVERAGES FROM 61 TO 220.

Thousands of bowlers participate in Moonlight Doubles, in which they bowl in a darkened environment. In 1943, the Franklin House Bowling Alleys had an early version of this concept. The only illumination in the building was at the scoring tables and the pin end of the alleys. Keeping with the times, what did they call their tournament?
A "BLACKOUT TOURNAMENT." EVEN THE PIT LIGHTS WERE SHADED WITH RED CLOTH.

In 1944, the U.S. government clamped down on bowling proprietors and demanded that all pin boys obtain one of these. What did the government require?

ALL PIN BOYS HAD TO OBTAIN SOCIAL SECURITY CARDS.

During the 1940's, you could buy a product called Shaafco Bowling Sandles. What was the purpose of these sandles?

THEY WOULD TAKE THE PLACE OF BOWLING SHOES BY BEING WORN OVER STREET SHOES WHILE BOWLING.

In August of 1944, Bowling Magazine, the official publication of the American Bowling Congress, featured a cover of past winners of various ABC tournaments. While this in itself was not unusual, what did each member of this featured group have in common?

THEY WERE ALL MEMBERS OF VARIOUS BRANCHES OF THE MILITARY.

From 1939 to 1944 there were 24 reported bowling alley fires throughout the U.S. Ten of these started under similar circumstances. What did these 10 fires have in common?

ALL WERE DETERMINED TO HAVE BEEN STARTED BY THE CARELESS SMOKING OF PIN BOYS.

There were 42 straight years of American Bowling Congress Tournaments before they were postponed. What led to the three-year postponement of this tournament?

WORLD WAR II.

Through the years, the American Bowling Congress passed many rules and regulations. In 1909, what did the ABC demand that each bowling team bring to the ABC tournament?

EACH *TEAM* HAD TO BRING AT LEAST ONE BOWLING BALL.

Another rule passed in 1924 was a prohibition against gambling-related companies. These companies were not allowed to do what?

THEY COULD NOT SPONSOR BOWLING TEAMS.

Also in 1928, gambling was prohibited in league and tournament bowling by the ABC. What punishment could participants caught violating this rule expect?

THEY COULD BE BARRED FROM COMPETING BECAUSE OF "MORAL DELINQUINCIES."

In 1933, gold, silver, and bronze rings were offered for the first time by the ABC for award scores. What type of awards were issued prior to the 1933 season?

PREVIOUS TO 1933, ONLY MEDALS WERE AVAILABLE FOR AWARDS.

In the autumn of 1942, a 10-team league was organized in Detroit. There was a specific criteria for joining this league. What was it?

THIS LEAGUE WAS ESTABLISHED FOR LEFT-HANDED BOWLERS ONLY.

Many people remember the famous headline that read "Dewey Defeats Truman" for the U.S. presidential election. What connection did Thomas Dewey have to bowling?
AS GOVERNOR OF NEW YORK, HE WELCOMED ALL PARTICIPANTS OF THE 1946 ABC TOURNAMENT IN BUFFALO, NEW YORK.

History tells us that the U.S. Army had a top secret program to develop an Atomic Bomb that was called the Manhattan Project. What could bowling possibly have to do with this nuclear project?
IN OAK RIDGE, TENNESSEE, A BRAND NEW EIGHT-LANE BOWLING CENTER WAS BUILT FOR THE INHABITANTS OF THIS CITY, WHO WERE QUARANTINED FROM LEAVING THE DEVELOPMENT BECAUSE OF SECURITY REASONS.

In Oak Ridge, also known as Atomic City, what action did bowlers take shortly after their bowling center was built?
THEY FORMED THEIR OWN CITY BOWLING ASSOCIATION.

As the A-bomb program expanded, how many total bowling centers were built for the inhabitants of the secret cities used in the atomic project?
FOUR BOWLING ESTABLISHMENTS WITH A TOTAL OF 36 LANES.

What former baseball player and manager bowled a 515 series in his debut as a participant in an ABC tournament held in Chicago, Illinois?
LOU BOUDREAU, WHO WAS A CHICAGO CUBS BASEBALL ANNOUNCER AT THE TIME.

Phil Rizzuto and Yogi Berra were partners in a New York bowling establishment. Can you name another baseball star who owned a center in Pennsylvania?

NELLIE FOX, BASEBALL'S MVP IN 1959.

What professional female bowler worked part time along with her daughter setting pins?

MARION LADEWIG.

In 1955, what major league baseball team placed a bowling lane on the baseball playing field for a bowling exposition?

CINCINNATI REDS.

What bowler appeared as the star of that exposition?

ANDY VERIPAPA.

What professional bowler spent four days in Vietnam visiting servicemen as part of a goodwill tour of the Orient?

DICK WEBER.

In July 1902, a magazine for women called the "Delineator" advised women to take up bowling for what reason?

THE MAGAZINE STATED THAT "A FEW HOURS OF BOWLING EACH WEEK WILL DO A WOMAN FULLY AS MUCH IF NOT MORE GOOD THAN ANY OTHER FORM OF EXERCISE."

What is the median age of a bowler in the U.S.?
27.6 YEARS.

Brunswick pinsetters are used throughout the world. Can you name this unique location of two lanes with Brunswick pinsetters, where they are reportedly used constantly by theology students?
IN THE BASEMENT OF THE VATICAN.

It is not documented whether Pope John Paul II has used these bowling lanes, but he has participated in this bowling variation. What game has he tried?
BOCCE.

In December 1981, the Jim Beam Distillery offered to donate a portion of the proceeds from the sale of their commemorative pin decanters to a specific cause. What did this donation benefit?
THE CONSTRUCTION OF THE NATIONAL BOWLING HALL OF FAME.

What former baseball great, as the head of the Presidents Council on Physical Fitness, was known to demonstrate his left handed bowling delivery?
STAN MUSIAL.

What function did a product known as the Bowler's Bucket serve? It even came with a three-fingered grip.
IT WAS AN ICE BUCKET IN THE SHAPE OF A BOWLING BALL.

FRAME 4:
A Good Day

How many consecutive "Brooklyn" strikes did Mary Sharp of Akron, Ohio knock down enroute to her 300 game?

MARY ROLLED 11 STRAIGHT BROOKLYNS BEFORE GETTING A POCKET HIT STRIKE ON HER LAST BALL IN THE TENTH FRAME.

Who was the first ambidextrous individual to bowl sanctioned 300 games both right-handed and left-handed?

GARY THOMPSON OF CALIFORNIA SHOT A RIGHT-HANDED 300 IN 1979, FOLLOWED BY A LEFT-HANDED 300 IN 1980.

What is the highest sanctioned three-game series that includes at least one game below 200?

A 799, BOWLED BY DON HARTLEY, FEATURED GAMES OF 300, 199, AND 300.

The record for consecutive duplicate games, or games of the same score, by an individual is seven. What was the repetitive score?

A SCORE OF 158 IN 1954.

Talk about shotmakers. Two men and one woman were able to consecutively string together a number of spares. How many did they successfully convert?

THIRTY IN A ROW.

Many bowlers strive for a perfect 300 game. One gentleman achieved this feat at the age of 86. Can you name him?

JOE NORRIS BOWLED A 300 IN 1994, TO BECOME THE OLDEST PERSON TO HAVE DONE SO.

Mr. Norris, a tremendous ambassador of bowling, also set another record with this perfect game. What was it?

HIS 67 YEARS BETWEEN PERFECT GAMES IS THE LONGEST SUCH SPAN.

While we're talking about super seniors, Ferdinand Georgie of Lansing, Michigan holds the record for highest three-game series for a senior. What was his series total?

AN 807 IN 1987

Carl Chavez of Albuquerque, New Mexico should have been devastated when he was left with four consecutive 6-7-10 splits. How many of these splits did he convert into spares?

ALL FOUR.

Dominic Scruci of Philadelphia could be called Mr. Consistency for accomplishing this feat five times in a row. What record did Dominic set during league play in 1943 that still stands today?

HE BOWLED FIVE CONSECUTIVE THREE-GAME SERIES OF 618.

A lot of people can bowl a score of twice their age. In fact, it does not sound that difficult. How old was Mollie Marler of Missouri when she bowled a score exactly twice her age?

SUPER SENIOR MOLLIE WAS 101 YEARS OLD WHEN SHE BOWLED A 202 GAME IN 1985.

The next time one of your bowling teammates calls at the last minute to say they can't make it, remind them of Nellie Marsura of Washington state. How many years did she bowl in her league without an absence?

FORTY-THREE YEARS.

Four men have each bowled at least two 800 series in competition. What was unique about two of the men that put them in the record books?

THEY WERE AMBIDEXTROUS, AND EACH BOWLED AN 800 USING EACH HAND.

Mike Randesi Jr. and Paul Cannon were bowling against each other in 1977 when they each bowled an 800 series to put them in the record books as the only opponents to do so. What else was unique about their accomplishment?

EACH WAS IN THE THIRD POSITION IN THEIR RESPECTIVE LINEUPS.

Linda Lunsford of Seattle enjoyed the holiday season in 1993 because of what consecutive bowling record?

SHE BOWLED SIX CONSECUTIVE 700 SERIES IN HER LEAGUE BEGINNING IN DECEMBER 1993.

Scott Owsley of Fontana, California is the youngest male to record a 300 game. He did so at the ripe old age of 10 in 1994. Who was the youngest female to accomplish this feat?

TRACY CASTRO, ALSO OF CALIFORNIA, BOWLED HER 300 GAME IN 1993 AT THE AGE OF 12.

Audrey Gable of Allentown, Pennsylvania bowled a 300 game the evening of April 30, 1988. What was unique about this event?

AUDREY WAS APPROXIMATELY EIGHT MONTHS PREGNANT AT THE TIME.

Al Laureys and his wife Mazey were the first husband and wife to bowl 300 games. Al bowled his in 1962, while Mazey accomplished hers a year later. Both were right handed. Who were the first left-handed husband and wife to bowl 300 games?

GERI AND DICK BEATTIE.

Linda Kelly bowled her first 300 game in 1981. Her husband, Bob, joined her with his own perfect game later that year. How many 300 games has this husband and wife team put in the record books?

SEVENTEEN. LINDA HAS EIGHT, BOB HAS NINE.

In 1953, Bill Phillips of Houston, Texas bowled a 300 game. Even though many had accomplished 300 games previously, what made this one unique?

IT WAS THE FIRST 300 GAME RECORDED ON AUTOMATIC PINSETTING EQUIPMENT DURING LEAGUE PLAY.

In the 1992–93 season, Rick Parsons of Lexington, Kentucky achieved a record that no one else can touch. What did he do 77 times in a row?

HE BOWLED 77 CONSECUTIVE 200 GAMES ON HIS WAY TO 104 FOR THE SEASON.

Roger Evans' average was 127 on April 12, 1991. Sometimes, everything goes your way. What did Roger accomplish that night?

HE HAD THE LOWEST AVERAGE OF ANY MALE TO THROW A 300 GAME.

During the 1932–33 season, Edward Mullen averaged 192. He did so, however, without accomplishing one of these. What was it?

EDWARD AVERAGED 192 WITHOUT BOWLING A 600 SERIES. HIS HIGHEST THAT SEASON WAS 599.

FRAME 5:
A Tough Night

What is the lowest three-game sanctioned series that includes a perfect 300 game?

IN 1989, REED TOWNLEY OF ALABAMA RECORDED GAMES OF 89, 87, AND 300 FOR A 476 SERIES.

Think your team is in a rut? How many years did the De Snyder Plasterettes team of Port Huron, Michigan use the same team lineup?

FORTY-ONE YEARS

John Prehm of New York holds the sanctioned record for the lowest game score in which a person bowled 11 strikes. What was his record-setting score?

TWO HUNDRED FORTY. JOHN BEGAN WITH THREE STRIKES, TOOK A ZERO IN THE FOURTH FRAME, AND THEN STRUCK OUT.

Splitsville? How many consecutive 7-10 splits did Payne Rose of St. Louis throw in 1962?

PAYNE THREW SIX CONSECUTIVE 7-10 SPLITS.

Before you feel too sorry for Payne, how many consecutive splits did Shirley Tophigh throw in Las Vegas during the 1968–69 season?

FOURTEEN STRAIGHT.

But even 14 straight pales in comparison to the number of splits that the Lengel Meat Packers men's team bowled during one game in 1955. Care to guess?

THIRTY-SEVEN SPLITS IN ONE GAME.

How many consecutive nine-pin counts did Pete Bland of Washington roll in 1976? (At least they weren't splits.)

EIGHTEEN NINE-PIN COUNTS.

The dreaded gutter ball. Mary Ellen Handley of Florida bowled the highest game on record that includes a gutter ball. What was Mary Ellen's score?

TWO HUNDRED, NINETY DURING THE 1980–81 SEASON.

Two men and two women have tied each other by scoring the highest game without a single spare or strike. What milestone score did they achieve without the benefit of a single mark?

90.

Everyone talks about pins over average. What is the record for pins *under* average for one game?

ANTHONY DELAHANDY OF ARIZONA ROLLED A 62 GAME WHILE CARRYING A 214 AVERAGE, FOR AN UNDER-AVERAGE SCORE OF 152.

Fouls happen to most bowlers occasionally, but what is the most fouls scored in one league game by an individual?

BUD MATHIESON COMMITTED 15 FOULS IN ONE GAME IN 1946. HE CONTINUED THAT PACE AND WOUND UP WITH 37 FOULS DURING HIS THREE-GAME SERIES.

Poor Richard Caplette of Conneticut managed to throw 19 gutter balls in one game in 1971. How many of these were consecutive?

NINE CONSECUTIVE CHANNEL BALLS ENROUTE TO HIS SINGLE-GAME RECORD.

If your bowling team is struggling to reach the 500 mark, consider the Men's Bible Class team from Pennsylvania. What is unique about their team's 1957–58 season?

THEY FINISHED THE SEASON WITH A COMBINED TEAM RECORD OF ONE WIN AND 139 LOSSES.

The 7-10 split receives a lot of notoriety, but the 8-10 is also very difficult. What is the record for most 8-10 splits in one three-game series?

JOHN ERMI MUST HAVE WANTED TO QUIT THE GAME WHEN HE WAS CREDITED WITH TWELVE 8-10 SPLITS IN 1937.

Harvey Lemons of Florida did not have split trouble. In fact, he bowled nine strikes during his game. However, he recorded the lowest sanctioned game bowled that included nine strikes. What was his score?

HARVEY BOWLED A 184.

FRAME 6:
Variations

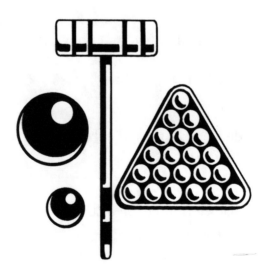

Skittles is a bowling game derived from which French game?
QUILLES.

In skittles, the wooden pins are also known as skittles. What is the wooden or rubber ball used in skittles referred to?
THE CHEESE.

How many pins are used in the game of skittles?
NINE.

In skittles, in what geometric shape are the pins placed?
DIAMOND.

What game originated in Italy and is sometimes known as lawn bowling?
BOCCE (ALSO SPELLED BOCCIE).

What is the diameter of the target ball used in bocce?
ONE AND ONE-HALF INCHES.

What is the diameter of the lob balls used in bocce?
FOUR AND ONE-HALF INCHES.

Kayles was an early version of bowling. In Kayles, a ball was not used to knock down pins. What was used?
STICKS OR CLUBS WERE USED TO KNOCK DOWN PINS.

Cloish was a game almost identical to Kayles except for one major difference. Do you know the basic difference between Kayles and Cloish?

A BALL REPLACED THE STICKS OR CLUBS TO KNOCK DOWN PINS.

Time for an easy question. Do you know the name of the sport played primarily in Canada that is sometimes referred to as "ice bowling?"

CURLING.

What game is being referred to when the "bowler" is attempting to throw the ball past the batsman to score points? (While doing this, the "bowler" is not supposed to bend their elbow.)

THE BRITISH GAME OF CRICKET.

Around 1540, the King of England granted licenses to certain gentlemen entitling them to play the game of skittles. What was the criteria for obtaining one of these licenses?

ONLY GENTLEMEN WITH HIGH INCOMES COULD RECEIVE A LICENSE.

Throughout the 1600's, ninepins was very popular. However, there were still many variations of the types of bowling games played. What country was known to have more types of bowling games than any other?

FRANCE.

In early variations of skittles, a kingpin was often part of the game. Why was a kingpin different than all other pins?

IN MANY CASES, A KINGPIN WOULD BE TALLER AND ALSO WORTH MORE POINTS THAN ANY OF THE OTHER PINS.

Another variation during the early days of bowling was known as Loggats. This game was extremely popular at sheep shearing festivals. What was unusual about the game of Loggats?

PARTICIPANTS USED ANIMAL BONES TO KNOCK DOWN PINS.

Q-Bowl was a table game version of tenpin bowling that was manufactured in Ohio. How did players of Q-Bowl knock down the miniature pins?

THEY SHOT A CUE BALL USING A BILLIARD CUE ACROSS A TABLE TO KNOCK DOWN MINIATURE BOWLING PINS.

In 1960, the Spare Time home bowling game was introduced. This game featured a magic slate score pad and cost only two dollars. What did this game utilize in place of bowling pins?

SPARE TIME WAS A DICE GAME IN WHICH EACH DIE REPRESENTED A BOWLING PIN.

What was the name of a home version bowling game created by the Wilson Sporting Goods Company in 1942? Why was it unique?

DART-BOWL WAS A HOME VERSION BOWLING GAME THAT WAS UNIQUE BECAUSE PLAYERS THREW DARTS AT A BOWLING DART BOARD TO SCORE POINTS.

In the 1960's, the Bally Company manufactured a pinball machine based on the game of bowling. What was the name of this pinball machine?

BOWL-O.

When the game of Duckpins was created in Baltimore around 1900, the balls used in competition were six inches in diameter. What is the diameter of a modern ball used in the game of duckpins?

FOUR AND SEVEN-EIGHTHS TO FIVE INCHES IN DIAMETER.

How did Duckpin bowling get its name?

JOHN MCGRAW AND WILBERT ROBINSON REMARKED THAT THE LITTLE PINS RESEMBLED FLYING DUCKS. THIS WAS PICKED UP IN A LOCAL NEWSPAPER STORY AND THE NAME STUCK.

One of the first ever Duckpin bowling centers was called the Diamond. What was unique about this establishment?

IT WAS A COMBINATION BAR, GYMNASIUM, AND TENPIN BOWLING ALLEY.

FRAME 7:
Bowling for Dollars

On March 2, 1985, which professional bowler lost $1 million by only four pins on national television?

PETE WEBER.

Why was he in the position to win a $1 million dollar bonus?

HE NEEDED TO WIN ALL THREE NATIONAL TOURNAMENTS SPONSORED BY THE MILLER BREWING COMPANY. HE HAD WON THE FIRST TWO TOURNAMENTS BEFORE LOSING IN THE FINAL MATCH OF THE THIRD.

Who defeated Weber in the title match to ruin his million dollar payday?

ERNIE SCHLEGEL.

Who was the first person to bowl a 300 game on television?

GRAZ CASTELLANO IN 1953 WHILE BOWLING FOR THE KRUEGER BEER TEAM.

Who was the captain of the Krueger Beer Team at the time?

ANDY VERIPAPA.

In 1946, Andy Veripapa won the All Star Tournament (today's U. S. Open). How old was he when he became the national champion?

FIFTY-FIVE YEARS OLD.

Who was the first man to ever repeat as national champion?
ANDY VERIPAPA.

Who were the first three bowlers in the Professional Bowlers Association to earn more than $100,000 in a single year?
EARL ANTHONY, MARK ROTH, AND MARSHALL HOLMAN.

Chris Schenkel and Nelson "Bo" Burton Jr. are the announcer and color commentator for the Professional Bowlers Tour on Television. Who was the color man that Bo Burton replaced?
BILLY WELU.

On July 1, 1982, what bowler astounded the bowling world with three perfect games, the first perfect 900 series recorded in 87 years?
GLEN ALLISON.

How many sanctioned 300 games had Glen Allison bowled prior to the night of this astounding performance?
FOUR.

What was the name of the bowling center in which Glen Allison bowled his perfect series?
LA HABRA 300 BOWL IN CALIFORNIA.

Glen bowled his 900 series while competing in a trio league. While much has been said about Glen's three-game series, what were the three-game series totals for each of his teammates on this historic night?

564 AND 467.

On March 12, 1958, the famous Budweiser Team bowled a then-record 3858 team series. Name the two members of this team who bowled perfect 300 games enroute to this score.

RAY BLUTH AND TOM HENNESSEY

Can you name the remaining members of the famous Budweiser team?

DON CARTER, DICK WEBER, AND PAT PATTERSON.

What leading money winner on the PBA tour discovered the "soaker" and used it to his advantage?

DON MCCUNE, WHO DISCOVERED THAT BY SOAKING A PLASTIC BOWLING BALL IN A CHEMICAL SOLUTION, THE BALL WOULD HAVE MORE TRACTION ON THE LANES.

What year was Don McCune the leading money winner and how much did he win?

IN 1973 HE WON $67,000.

Who was the first winner of the inaugural High Roller Tournament in Las Vegas?

MICK MORTON.

How much did Mick Morton win in that first High Roller?

$210,000.

What PBA bowler used to stick his sore thumb in a potato to help it heal?

DON JOHNSON.

In 1977, Mark Roth won four PBA titles and more than $100,000 on the tour in prize money. How much did he win his first year on the PBA tour?

A LITTLE OVER $1,000.

What was the first year the Pro Bowler's tour was televised on Saturday afternoons?

1962.

Chris Schenkel has been the voice of Saturday afternoon telecasts of the Pro Bowler's Tour since its inception. Name two movies in which Chris had acting roles.

CHRIS APPEARED IN "REQUIEM FOR A HEAVYWEIGHT," AND "NATIONAL VELVET."

How did PBA bowler Mark Baker get the nickname "Moon?"

WHILE BOWLING ON NATIONAL TELEVISION DURING A TOURNAMENT, HIS PANTS SPLIT, REVEALING HE WASN'T WEARING ANY UNDERWEAR.

You will never guess the popular city in which this
"mooning" incident occurred.
MIAMI.

Famous bowler Ned Day had an unusual superstition. What
was it?
HE WOULD NOT SHAKE HANDS WITH ANYONE FOR FEAR OF
INJURING HIS BOWLING HAND.

Who were the first father and son duo to be elected to the
American Bowling Congress Hall of Fame?
NELSON BURTON SR. AND NELSON BURTON JR.

In 1959, how much money did the leading money winner on
the professional bowlers tour earn?
DICK WEBER WON $7,672.

How much did the leading money winner on the professional
tour earn in 1993?
WALTER RAY WILLIAMS JR. WON $296,370.

What is the record for earnings won in a single PBA season?
MIKE AULBY WON $298,237 IN 1989.

Who won the inaugural Firestone Tournament of
Champions in 1965, which featured a $100,000 prize fund?
BILLY HARDWICK, WHO WON $25,000 FOR HIS FIRST PLACE FINISH.

What PBA member holds the record for the most 200 games in succession?

IN 1993, WALTER RAY WILLIAMS BOWLED 61 CONSECUTIVE 200 GAMES IN TOURNAMENT PLAY.

What PBA member holds the record for most PBA tournament titles in one year?

MARK ROTH WON EIGHT TOURNAMENTS IN 1978.

Two other PBA members have each won seven tournaments in one year. Who are they?

WALTER RAY WILLIAMS IN 1993 AND EARL ANTHONY IN 1975.

In 1994, PBA member Norm Duke bowled the highest losing score on national television during a PBA tournament. What was his losing score?

280.

Who beat Norm Duke and what score did he bowl?

BRYAN GOEBEL SHOT 296 TO DEFEAT DUKE'S 280.

What PBA bowler was the first to bowl a perfect 300 game on national television during a PBA tournament?

JACK BIONDOLILLO IN AKRON OHIO IN 1967.

What was the combined total of perfect games that Earl Anthony and Mark Roth have bowled on national television?

ZERO.

What PBA member had the highest single-season earnings while never winning a tournament?

PETE MCCORDIC WON $156,476 IN 1987.

Who bowled 14 consecutive years with at least one title on the PBA tour?

EARL ANTHONY (1970–83).

Who was the youngest player to win a PBA tournament?

NORM DUKE WAS JUST 18 YEARS OLD IN 1983.

Who was the oldest player to win a PBA tournament?

BUZZ FAZIO WAS 56 WHEN HE WON IN SACRAMENTO IN 1965.

What Hall of Famer won three of the first four PBA tournaments ever held?

DICK WEBER.

In what year was the first Senior PBA tournament held?

THE INAUGURAL PBA SENIOR CHAMPIONSHIP WAS HELD IN 1981.

Who won the 1981 PBA Senior Championship?

ABC HALL OF FAMER BILL BEACH.

What are the requirements to be eligible for PBA membership?

A MINIMUM AVERAGE OF 190 OVER THE TWO MOST RECENT ABC SANCTIONED SEASONS IN LEAGUES OF 66 OR MORE GAMES.

How many charter members were there when the Professional Bowlers Association was founded in 1958?

THIRTY THREE.

Earl Anthony holds the record for all-time PBA tournament wins with 41. Who is second?

MARK ROTH WITH 34 TITLES.

Which professional female bowler holds the career record for most title victories?

LISA WAGNER WITH 28.

As of December 1994, four women professional bowlers have eclipsed the $500,000 mark in career earnings. Can you name them?

ROBIN ROMEO, TISH JOHNSON, LISA WAGNER, AND ALETA SILL.

What is the highest scoring TV match between professional female bowlers?

FIVE HUNDRED FIFTY-FIVE PINS. LEANNE BARRETTE DEFEATED ALETA SILL 279 TO 276 IN 1988.

Johnny Petraglia, in 1971, and Mark Roth, in 1977, each won three consecutive professional bowling tournaments. What professional won three consecutive tournaments three different times?

DICK WEBER IN 1959, 1960, AND 1961.

Seven women bowlers have won the U.S. Open championship twice in their careers. Can you name the woman who has won this championship eight times?

MARION LADEWIG.

Who was the first woman bowler to earn $100,000 in a single season?

LISA WAGNER WON $105,500 IN 1988.

In 1965, Dick Weber led professional bowlers with $47,675 in prize money won. During that same year, how much did the leading women's professional earn?

BETTY KUCZYNSKI WON $3,792.

In 1983, Earl Anthony won the last of his record-setting six selections as PBA Player of the Year. Who was selected as the Ladies Professional Bowler's Tour Bowler of the Year in 1983?

LISA RATHGEBER.

In 1923, the Peterson Tournament paid out a total of $5,600 in prize money. How much did the first-place winner receive?

$2,000.

What was the individual entry fee for this tournament the following year?

$25.

The George London Dream Tourney was a unique bowling tournament that had a sizable prize fund in 1958. What was the total value of the prizes offered that year?

$50,000 IN 1958.

Johnny King won the inaugural George London Tournament in Chicago in 1956. What was the criteria for entering this tournament?

YOU MUST HAVE BOWLED A PERFECT GAME IN ABC SANCTIONED COMPETITION WHILE WEARING A GEORGE LONDON BOWLING SHIRT.

The 1958 tournament offered an automobile as a prize. What type of automobile could you have won?

A PLYMOUTH BELVEDERE HARD TOP.

One of the earliest known bowling competitions in France was a winner-take-all tournament. What entry fee did each participant have to supply?

A CHICKEN. THE WINNER WOULD RECEIVE ALL THE CHICKENS.

That's nothing. Tournaments in Germany and Poland around the year 1500 also paid prizes in livestock. What did the winner receive in each country?

IN GERMANY THE PRIZE WAS A DEER, WHILE IN POLAND THE WINNER TOOK HOME AN OX.

FRAME 8:
Equipment Then and Now

A modern bowling ball cannot exceed the maximum allowable weight of 16 pounds. What is the minimum allowable weight?

THERE IS NO MINIMUM.

Many modern bowling balls use this material as part of the core. Can you guess the material?

LIMESTONE.

In the modern game of bowling, 10 pins are arranged in a triangle. What is the distance between each pin?

EACH PIN IS 12 INCHES AWAY FROM THE NEXT PIN.

What two types of wood have been used extensively to manufacture bowling lanes?

MAPLE AND PINE.

What was the purpose of a "two way" bowling ball?

BETWEEN 1930 AND 1940 THIS HOUSEBALL HAD TWO DIFFERENT SIZE GRIPS THAT COULD BE USED BY EITHER MEN OR WOMEN.

What would have been the heaviest legal weight of that bowling ball in 1902?

EIGHTEEN POUNDS.

What was your 1902 vintage 18 pound bowling ball made of? (Here's a hint: *Lignum vitae* is the Latin term for this common substance.)

WOOD.

What type of bowling ball was used by Earl Anthony when he became the first bowler to win $100,000 in prize money during a single season?

AN EBONITE MAGNUM VI.

What is the diameter of a modern bowling ball?

EIGHT AND ONE-HALF INCHES.

Everyone throws an occasional gutter ball. Knowing that the circumference of a bowling ball is approximately 27 inches, what is the depth of a lane gutter at its deepest point?

AT LEAST ONE AND SEVEN-EIGHTHS INCHES AT THE CENTER.

On a bowling lane, there are several dots or aiming points between the foul line and the arrows. These are sometimes known as cherries. What is the total number of cherries on a bowling lane?

THERE ARE 10 DOTS OR CHERRIES SEVEN FEET FROM THE FOUL LINE.

In 1936, the Brunswick Corporation introduced their "20TH Century" line of bowling equipment, which was colorful and streamlined. Besides being aesthetically pleasing, what did this new equipment hide from the bowler's vision?

A SCREEN HID THE PIN BOYS FROM VIEW. THIS WAS AN EARLY VERSION OF TODAY'S MASKING UNITS.

Before limestone, this material was used as a core for many bowling balls. What was it?

SAWDUST.

Many golfers are familiar with the durability of some types of golf balls. Can you name the surface material that is used on both golf balls and certain bowling pins?

SURLYN.

In 1923, for what price could you purchase a new Ebonite bowling ball?

THEY WERE $14 EACH WITH NO PRICE VARIATION FOR EITHER A TWO OR THREE FINGERED BALL.

Bowling proprietors could purchase a set of 10 bowling pins for $5 in 1923. How much does a set of pins cost today?

IN EXCESS OF $100 PER SET OF 10.

Let's not forget about bowling shoes. During the 1920's, what could you expect to pay for a pair of bowling shoes?

$4.65 PER PAIR.

The gutter sections located at the pin area of a bowling lane next to the pin deck are a unique shape in contrast to the rest of the gutters. What shape are they?

FLAT, AS OPPOSED TO CONCAVE.

What was the weight of the original robotic pin setting machine?

TWO THOUSAND POUNDS.

In 1958, you could purchase men's and women's broadcloth bowling shirts for $4.95 each. How much were these shirts if you chose to have them made of gabardine?

$6.95.

If you wanted to purchase a brand-new bowling ball in 1902, what would you have expected to pay?

ABOUT $4.25.

What was unique about the Triangle Sep-a-Rator bowling bag that set it apart from its competition?

THIS BAG FEATURED A SEPARATE COMPARTMENT FOR YOUR BOWLING SHOES, AWAY FROM YOUR BOWLING BALL.

In 1958, a new piece of bowling equipment was introduced by the Chicago Hardware Foundry Company called a Sani-Dry. What was the purpose of the Sani-Dry?

A SANI-DRY WAS A PATENTED ELECTRIC HAND DRYER THAT WAS MOUNTED ON THE BALL RETURNS.

What was the distinct shape of the Sani-Dry machine?

IT RESEMBLED A BOWLING BALL.

The Brunswick Corporation reached a sales milestone in 1959. What piece of equipment had reached the pinnacle of twenty thousand sold by 1959?

THEIR 20,000TH AUTOMATIC PINSETTER WAS INSTALLED IN A BOWLING CENTER IN CONNETICUT.

Why would men bowling in the 1950's want to wear Don Carter Bowling Slacks?

BECAUSE THEY HAD THE HIDDEN STRETCH WAISTBAND.

In 1966, a bowling accessory called a Tele-Strike was introduced that you could wear on your wrist as you bowled. What was the intended purpose of this product?

THIS $3.95 ITEM WAS DESIGNED TO GIVE YOU INSTANT FEEDBACK ABOUT WHAT YOU WERE DOING WRONG IN YOUR DELIVERY AND HOW YOU COULD CORRECT IT.

When wooden bowling lanes or alleys were first used, bowlers rolled the ball on a bare wood surface. Shellac was then used as a lane coating. What were the drawbacks of using shellac?

SHELLAC WAS VERY SOFT AND THE BALL TRACK AREA WORE OUT EVERY TWO TO THREE WEEKS. THEREFORE, RECOATING HAD TO BE DONE OFTEN, CHANGING THE LANE SURFACE.

What other types of lane finishes followed the use of shellac?

LACQUER, URETHANE, WATER BASED, AND SYNTHETICS.

During the 1900's, cork balls were made of lightweight pressed wood. Composition balls followed these and were similar except for one variation. What improvement was made with a composition ball?

THEY WERE BASICALLY CORK BALLS COVERED WITH A HARD RUBBER COATING.

During the early years of outdoor bowling, bowlers often set their pins on wood slabs or flat stones. Later, three different substances were used to create smoother, more level lanes. What were the substances?

CLAY, CINDERS, AND SLATE.

How many aiming arrows are on a bowling lane?

SEVEN.

A product that originated in Tennessee was called the "Alley Cat." This product reportedly eliminated the need to scrub the soles of bowling shoes with steel wool. What was the "Alley Cat?"

AN AUTOMATIC SHOE CLEANER DESIGNED FOR PLACEMENT WITHIN BOWLING CENTERS. JUST DROP FIVE CENTS IN THE COIN SLOT AND YOU RECEIVED 25 SECONDS OF CLEANING POWER.

Before electricity, what lighting method was used to illuminate bowling lanes?

GASLIGHTS.

Before the use of scoresheets, how did bowlers keep score?

SCORES WERE WRITTEN ON SLATE BOARDS WITH CHALK.

Chalk was also used in bowling alleys for a another, very different purpose. For what other function was chalk used in a bowling center?

BOXES OF CHALK WERE MOUNTED AT FLOOR LEVEL NEXT TO THE ALLEYS SO THAT BOWLERS COULD RUB THE SOLES OF THEIR SHOES IN IT TO IMPROVE TRACTION.

Before ball returns were automated, how did they work?

PINBOYS WOULD SHOVE THE BALL DOWN A RAMP THAT WOULD END UP ON A RACK IN THE BOWLERS AREA. PINBOYS WHO WERE UNHAPPY ABOUT THE VELOCITY OF A BOWLER'S DELIVERY WOULD SOMETIMES RETURN THEM EXTRA HARD SO THEY WOULD FALL OFF THE RACKS.

Electronic foul detectors were a much-welcomed invention to the bowling industry. How were fouls determined before they were invented?

A FOUL JUDGE WOULD SIT ON A RAISED STOOL AND MANUALLY CALL FOULS ALONG HIS LINE OF SIGHT. AS YOU CAN IMAGINE, THIS SOMETIMES RESULTED IN HEATED ARGUMENTS.

A "Bowl Handl" (sic) was an amazing device that delivered a bowling ball without using the finger holes. Rubber suction cups were used to pick up the ball. In what year was this $80 product available?

1960.

The Kegeltron was also available in 1960. The Kegeltron was known as a "framemaster automatic totalizer." For what purpose was it used?

THE KEGELTRON WAS A MACHINE DESIGNED FOR BOWLING PROPRIETORS TO METER THE TOTAL AMOUNT OF FRAMES BOWLED DURING A BUSINESS DAY.

What is the circumference of a modern bowling ball?

MINIMUM CIRCUMFERENCE IS 26.704 INCHES NOT TO EXCEED 27.002 INCHES.

How tall is a modern regulation bowling pin?

FIFTEEN INCHES.

FRAME 9:
Advertisements

If you chose not to wear a George London shirt while bowling, you could choose a Service bowling shirt. What unique claim did a Service bowling shirt make?

THE SERVICE BOWLING SHIRTS CORPORATION EXPLAINED THAT THEIR SHIRTS WERE SANITIZED FOR LASTING FRESHNESS AND WERE THE BOWLING SHIRTS WITH THE BUILT IN DEODORANT.

During the year 1963, baseball great Yogi Berra appeared in a publicity photo standing in a batter's box preparing to hit. Bowling star Buddy Bomar was the pitcher. Can you name the personality who was the catcher for this unique photo?

MARION LADEWIG WAS THE "STAR" CATCHER IN THIS PICTURE.

Mickey Rooney, Alice Fay, Ginger Rogers, and Ronald Coleman were all pictured bowling together in the 1940's. What was the occasion of this star studded bowling event?

MGM STUDIOS SPONSORED A BOWLING PARTY.

What was the title of a bowling magazine widely distributed in Japan during the 1970's?

"TOP BOWLER."

What bowling ball manufacturer's advertising slogan was "the ball that bowls right"?

EBONITE.

In 1925, how much would you expect to pay for home delivery of a national bowling magazine?

FIVE CENTS PER WEEK FOR 52 WEEKS.

If you owned a Brunswick-Balke-Collander Mineralite bowling ball, what did their advertising claim?

USING THEIR EQUIPMENT ESTABLISHED YOU AS A LEADER.

In 1933, what transportation company used the advertising jingle "Merrily we bowl along… to the tournament or anywhere"?

GREYHOUND LINES.

In 1941, the magazine "The Woman Bowler" included an advertisement for a bowling ball that was called "The Ball of Champions!" Who was the manufacturer of this ball?

THIS CAME FROM THE BOWLING BALL DEPARTMENT OF THE
MANHATTAN RUBBER MANUFACTURING CO.

What company's advertisement advised to bowlers "Get in the groove and stay there with 33 to 1"?

PABST BLUE RIBBON BEER, WHICH WAS BLENDED FROM 33 FINE
BREWS.

In 1958, what baseball-star-turned-bowling-proprietor endorsed Brunswick Automatic Pinsetters?

NEW YORK YANKEE GREAT YOGI BERRA.

What was the name of Yogi Berra's bowling center that was located in New Jersey?

BERRA-RIZZUTO BOWLING LANES, WHICH YOGI CO-OWNED WITH PARTNER AND FELLOW BASEBALL PLAYER PHIL RIZZUTO.

During the Christmas gift-giving season of 1958, what was included with the purchase of any Ebonite Tornado or Satellite bowling ball?

FREE GIFT WRAPPING THAT INCLUDED CRIMSON COLORED RIBBON.

If you drank a beverage that was advertised as "The perfect way to top your game," what would you be drinking?

FALSTAFF BEER.

What breakfast cereal featured a "Bowling Champions" contest that you could win by submitting a finishing verse to a bowling jingle that was on the box?

WHEATIES.

What was the top prize for winning the Wheaties contest?

$20,000.

Hall of Fame bowler Billy Welu offered personal bowling instruction by mail in 1960 for $4.98 post paid, what type of instructions would you receive?
YOU WOULD HAVE RECEIVED IN THE MAIL A 33 1/3 LP RECORD BY MR. WELU ENTITLED STRIKE.

The Ebonite bowling ball company advertised in the 1960's that a chemical put "Steam" in the ball you roll. What substance was included in their bowling ball formula?
SULPHUR.

What bowling ball advertised in the 1960's was said to have "Thrust" and also that "extra Mix?"
COLUMBIA 300.

FRAME 10:
Miscellania

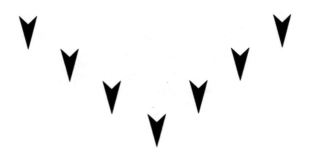

How much did Detroit bowler Therm Gibson win for throwing six consecutive strikes in 1961 while bowling on the television show "Jackpot Bowling?"

GIBSON WON $75,000. AS AN EXAMPLE OF HOW LARGE A PAYOUT THIS WAS, GARY PLAYER WAS THE LEADING MONEY WINNER ON THE PRO GOLF TOUR THAT YEAR. HE WON $64,540.00 FOR THE ENTIRE SEASON.

What world-famous artist was commissioned $50,000 to paint a bowling-themed portrait?

LEROY NEIMAN.

What is the title of this painting?

THE MILLION DOLLAR STRIKE.

What PBA Hall of Fame bowler is depicted bowling on this painting? Who else appears?

EARL ANTHONY. FELLOW HALL OF FAMERS ANDY VERIPAPA, DON CARTER, AND NELSON BURTON JR. ARE ALSO FEATURED IN THE BACKGROUND.

Where is the original painting now on display?

AT THE NATIONAL BOWLING HALL OF FAME.

In what midwestern city is the National Bowling Hall of Fame located?

ST. LOUIS, MISSOURI.

On what date was the ground breaking ceremony for the National Bowling Hall of Fame held?

APRIL 20, 1982.

What well-known sports arena is located across the street from the National Bowling Hall of Fame?

BUSCH STADIUM.

What Olympic gold medalist was a spokesperson for bowling in 1985?

MARY LOU RETTON.

Which future U.S. President was featured on the cover of "Bowler's Journal" magazine in 1946? His wife appeared with him. Who was she?

RONALD REAGAN APPEARED WITH FIRST WIFE JANE WYMAN.

Which left-handed U.S. President was featured on the cover of "The National Kegler" magazine in 1947?

PRESIDENT HARRY TRUMAN.

This gentleman pro bowler was one of the first bowlers to write an instruction book on the sport. "How to Bowl" was a huge success. Who wrote this book?

NED DAY.

"How to Bowl" was the first sports instruction book to use what as a teaching method?
SEQUENCE PHOTOGRAPHY.

How can a bowling pin be a messenger?
A PIN THAT ROLLS ACROSS THE LANE AND TAKES DOWN ANOTHER PIN IS REFERRED TO AS A MESSENGER.

What is it called when a bowler does not get a spare or a strike in a frame?
THAT FRAME IS CONSIDERED AN OPEN FRAME.

What is another term for a gutter ball?
A CHANNEL BALL.

What is a Dutch 200 game?
A SCORE RESULTING FROM ALTERNATING SPARES AND STRIKES WITH A SCORE OF TWENTY IN EACH FRAME.

Which pin is sometimes known as the kingpin?
THE FIVE PIN.

What is spot bowling?
AIMING AT A SPOT OR MARK ON THE LANES INSTEAD OF AIMING BY LOOKING AT THE PINS.

What is a Jersey strike?

ANOTHER NAME FOR A BROOKLYN STRIKE.

What is considered dead wood?

DOWNED PINS THAT REMAIN ON A LANE AFTER A HIT ARE CALLED DEAD WOOD.

Dick Weber has traveled the world promoting bowling. He has put on demonstrations in many unique places, including intermissions at rodeos. None may have been as unusual as his promotional match against women's champion Silvia Wene. Where was this match located?

ON BOARD A JET AIRPLANE IN FLIGHT.

Appendix

SCORING LOG

	Date	Game 1	Game 2	Game 3	Total Pins	Total	Average
1							
2							
3							
4							
5							
6							
7							
8							
9							
10							
11							
12							
13							
14							
15							
16							
17							
18							
19							
20							
21							
22							
23							
24							
25							
26							
27							
28							
29							
30							
31							
32							
33							
34							
35							
36							

BOWLING TIPS

Grip

Of the three basic grips in bowling, the conventional grip is recommended for the beginners and is widely used by most average bowlers.

A bowler should choose a ball so the hand fits into the ball without gripping the ball too tightly or stretching the hand in order to hold the ball.

Stance

Position of the feet is a key factor of the stance. If a bowler is right-handed, the left foot should be extended forward a bit, perpendicular to the foul line. Lefthanders, do the opposite. The knees should be bent slightly. The shoulders should be square to the foul line and the body should lean forward slightly.

The bowling ball should be held somewhere between the knees and chin, at the point that is the most comfortable for the bowler. the weight of the ball should be in the non-bowling ball hand.

What the bowler does in the stance will affect all other movements made up to the point of delivery. The entire process must be fluid, from stance to follow through.

Approach

A four step approach is recommended for beginners. Lefthanders reverse these left-right directions:

- Start with the right foot. At the same time push the ball away keeping it to the right side of the body so that a straight backswing and forward swing will result.
- The second step, made with the left foot, is at the point when the ball is at the bottom of the backswing.
- The third step, made with the right foot forward, is also the time when the ball is at the height of the backswing. Keep the shoulders square, and lean towards the foul line.

Delivery

The delivery is getting the ball from the bowler's hand to the pins. Do not drop the ball or throw it. Gently lay it down on the lane from three to twelve inches from the foul line.

At the point of releasing the ball over the foul line the bowler should find their fingers in the ball and the thumb out. The thumb MUST come out first for a proper release. To give the ball a spinning action a slight lift of the fingers should be made upon release.

The delivery hand should continue up in a hand shaking position for a correct follow-through.

Scoring

These are the symbols that make up the bowling shorthand:

$$\boxed{\times} \qquad \boxed{/} \qquad \boxed{0} \qquad \boxed{-}$$

A game consists of ten frames. Each box on the scoresheet represents one frame.

1	2	3	4	5	6	7	8	9	10
9 /	9 —	X	X	5 /	7 —	X	6 —	8 /	X /
19	28	53	73	90	97	113	119	139	159

Two balls are bowled in each frame unless a strike is rolled. A strike occurs when all ten pins are knocked down with the first ball of the frame. All ten pins knocked down with the two allotted balls of the frame constitutes a spare.

If the bowler fails to knock down all ten pins with two balls, they simply record the total number of pins downed, and add the total to the score for the previous frame.

1	2	3	4	5	6	7	8	9	10
9 /	9 —	X	X	5 /	7 —	X	6 —	8 /	X /
19	28	53	73	90	97	113	119	139	159

If the bowler strikes, the score for that frame is TEN plus the number of pins knocked down by the next TWO balls.

1	2	3	4	5	6	7	8	9	10
9 /	9 —	☒	☒	5 /	7 — ☒	6 —	8 /	☒	/
19	28	53	73	90	97	113	119	139	159

If the bowler spares, the score is TEN plus the number of pins knocked down with the FIRST ball in the next frame.

If a strike is made in the 10th frame, the bowler must roll two additional balls. For a spare in the 10th frame, one extra ball. The maximum number of balls you can roll in the 10th frame is three.

1	2	3	4	5	6	7	8	9	10
9 /	9 —	☒	☒	5 /	7 — ☒	6 —	8 /	☒	/
19	28	53	73	90	97	113	119	139	159

The score is carried forward in each frame and the tenth will show the bowler's final score.

Spares

A bowler can roll as high as 190 without ever getting a strike, if all spares are made. The important factor in making a spare is the ANGLE. Spares should be shot from the opposite side of the approach- if a spare is to the right, stand to the left, and if the spare is to the left, stand to the right.

HEAD PIN SPARES are shot from the strike position. Adjust the angle of the approach depending on the combination of pins in the spare.

TWO PIN SPARES such as the 6-10 or 1-3 are made by aiming between the two pins. Where the pins stand directly behind one another, such as the 2-8 or 3-9, a good solid hit on the front pin is essential. In all spares it is important to hit as many pins as you can with the ball rather than knocking the pins into each other.

Splits

A split occurs when after rolling the first ball, at least two pins remain standing that are not adjacent to each other, with the head pin down.

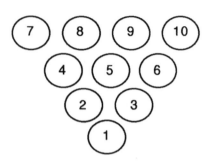

FIT-IN SPLITS such as the 4-5, 5-6, 7-8, 9-10, are made by trying to fit the ball between them. Aim and timing are important here.

BABY SPLITS such as the 2-7, or 3-10, are made by shooting cross-angles, aiming for the space between the pins.

Wider splits such as the 5-7 or 4-10 can be made by sliding the 4 or 5 pin across into either the 7 or 10 pin. It is good strategy to shoot for one pin when you have splits such as the 7-10, 8-10, or the 4-6.

Etiquette

- Remember, a five member team is allocated 45 minutes to complete ONE GAME. Avoidable delays hurt your team and all other bowlers scheduled behind you.
- Respect the equipment. Wait for the pinsetting machine to complete its cycle before releasing your ball. LOFTING THE BALL HURTS YOUR GAME AND DAMAGES THE LANE.
- Good bowling requires concentration. Provide your fellow bowlers the same courtesy you desire when it is your turn to bowl.
- When two people are ready to bowl on adjoining lanes, the bowler on the RIGHT has the right of way to bowl first.

ORDER FORM

Use this convenient coupon for ordering additional copies of
The Bowling Trivia Book!

Please send me _____ copies of "The Bowling Trivia Book."

I am enclosing $6.95 for each book, plus $2.00 to cover postage
and handling. Send check or money order (no cash or COD's
accepted). Canadian residents enclose $8.95 per book plus $2.00
to cover postage.

Name _____

Address _____

City _____ State _____ Zip _____

For information on quantity pricing, please write to the address
below or call 1-810-347-1350. Please allow 2–3 weeks for
delivery.

Mail to:

WMS Bowling Group
42240 Grand River Ave.
Suite 202
Novi, Michigan 48375-1836